This Journal Belongs to

Cakes n Candles

Cakes n Candles

Made in United States
Troutdale, OR
08/08/2023

11925252R00072